Train Your Brain

with **Parallel Computing** and **If/Then Activities**

by **Emilee Hillman**

illustrated by **Dana Regan**

Published in 2020 by Cavendish Square Publishing, LLC
243 5th Avenue, Suite 136, New York, NY 10016

Website: cavendishsq.com

This publication represents the opinions and views of the author based on his or her personal
experience, knowledge, and research. The information in this book serves as a general
guide only. The author and publisher have used their best efforts in preparing this book and
disclaim liability rising directly or indirectly from the use and application of this book.

All websites were available and accurate when this book was sent to press.

Library of Congress Cataloging-in-Publication Data

Names: Hillman, Emilee, author.
Title: Train your brain with parallel computing and if/then activities / Emilee Hillman.
Description: First edition. | New York, NY : Cavendish Square Publishing, LLC, 2020. | Series: Think
like a programmer | Includes bibliographical references and index. | Audience: Grades 2 to 5.
Identifiers: LCCN 2018059295 (print) | LCCN 2018061553 (ebook) | ISBN 9781502648211 (ebook) |
ISBN 9781502648204 (library bound) | ISBN 9781502648181 (pbk.) | ISBN 9781502648198 (6 pack)
Subjects: LCSH: Parallel programming (Computer science)--Juvenile literature. |
Conditionals (Logic)--Juvenile literature.
Classification: LCC QA76.642 (ebook) | LCC QA76.642 .H555 2020 (print) | DDC 005.2/75--dc23
LC record available at https://lccn.loc.gov/2018059295

Editorial Director: David McNamara
Editor: Kristen Susienka
Copy Editor: Nathan Heidelberger
Associate Art Director: Alan Sliwinski
Designer: Joe Parenteau
Illustrator: Dana Regan
Production Coordinator: Karol Szymczuk

Printed in the United States of America

Contents

INTRODUCTION 4

GROUP LUNCH 6

CLEANING HOUSE 8

MUSIC IN PARALLEL 10

WORKING TOGETHER 12

HIDDEN OBJECTS 14

PEEK AND COPY 16

CONDITIONAL DIET 18

COLOR CHANGE 20

SIMON CONDITIONALLY SAYS 22

IF I WRITE A STORY 24

ROLLING CONDITIONALS 26

CHARACTER IF/THEN 28

GLOSSARY 30

FIND OUT MORE 31

INDEX 32

Introduction

You want to be a computer programmer—great! The best programmers understand how to put ideas together and test results many times. They also know how to give and follow instructions. Some of the most important instructions are **if/then statements**. They are also called **conditionals**. If/then statements help tell a computer how to do a job. The activities in this book will help you understand if/then statements in computer programming. They will also help you understand other ideas like **parallel computing**, working together, and using creativity to get tasks done.

This is all part of **computational thinking**. Despite the name, this way of thinking doesn't need a computer! All you have to do is think about how to solve problems, one step at a time.

These fun activities will help you train your brain to organize information to solve a bigger problem, to tackle if/then statements, and to finish tasks

with help from others. You'll also learn that some solutions work well while others don't. That is why it's important to understand and practice this thinking. This is how you learn to think like a programmer!

Group Lunch

NUMBER OF PLAYERS 2

TIME NEEDED

20–30 minutes

ACTIVITY OVERVIEW

Good computational thinkers can break a problem into several parts that happen at the same time. This is called parallel computing. Sometimes it is called parallelism. It is named that because different things will be running in parallel, or at the same time. In this activity, you and a friend will practice parallel computing with food.

INSTRUCTIONS

First, you and your friend should work together. Choose a simple lunch. Some ideas are a grilled cheese, a salad, or a peanut butter and jelly sandwich. Then, work together to come up with a way to make that lunch together! How will you work together to quickly prepare the food? Take turns writing or drawing the actions for making the meal. To speed things up, can you do one task while your friend does another? Later, to practice more, try actually making your lunch by following the steps you created.

Cleaning House

NUMBER OF PLAYERS

TIME NEEDED

15–20 minutes

ACTIVITY OVERVIEW

Parallel computing is one way programmers can use **code** to its greatest potential. It also helps if the code is simple and easy to follow. This is called **efficient**. Efficient code works well. It also helps a program run more smoothly. Often, parallel computing helps a program be efficient. In this activity, you will learn to do chores efficiently.

INSTRUCTIONS

To begin, think about cleaning the house. What different chores do you have to do to get it clean? Next, draw or write a plan to clean the house. You should include other family members to help. Each

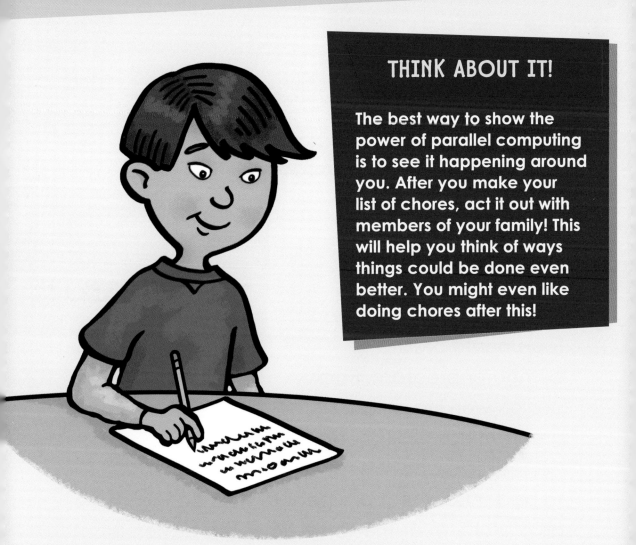

THINK ABOUT IT!

The best way to show the power of parallel computing is to see it happening around you. After you make your list of chores, act it out with members of your family! This will help you think of ways things could be done even better. You might even like doing chores after this!

person should work at the same time, in parallel. Each person should also get the same amount of work. For example, give the same number of chores to everyone. This will help you keep things organized.

9

Music in Parallel

NUMBER OF PLAYERS **3 OR MORE**

TIME NEEDED

20–30 minutes

ACTIVITY OVERVIEW

Often, many people work together to create a computer program. Each person working on the program has a different perspective and skill set to add. Also, the more people who can work on a problem at the same time, the better. In this activity, you and some friends will practice parallelism by making music.

INSTRUCTIONS

Ask some friends to join you in this activity! Once there is a group of three or more players, listen to a song that has both instruments and people singing. Notice how the instruments and voices work at the same time to make the song come together?

Next, you and your friends should try to put a song together yourselves. Everyone should pick a part. For example, one person could clap a pattern, one person could snap their fingers, one person could stomp their feet, and one person could hum a simple **melody**.

Decide on a basic pattern to follow for your song. Each person should practice their part individually. Once everyone has their part mastered, work together. The parts you practiced should come together to make the song.

Working Together

NUMBER OF PLAYERS ①

TIME NEEDED

15–20 minutes

ACTIVITY OVERVIEW

Parallelism helps make difficult work look easy. The more people who work on a task, the quicker the task is finished. Computational thinkers know this. They always try to find ways for different parts of their code to work at the same time. In this activity, you will practice real-life parallelism.

INSTRUCTIONS

To start, write down a list of activities. These activities should be ones that need many people working together at the same time. Some examples are: team sports, putting on a play, a choir, or an orchestra. After you have a list of activities, draw a picture showing how people work at the same time for each activity. You should try to make each drawing show the people working together!

THINK ABOUT IT!

Parallel computing can be tricky to learn. It's hard to keep track of so many moving pieces! To build on this activity, get together with some friends. Together, act out some of the activities you listed. For example, you could invite some friends over to play football. As you're playing, think about how impossible it would be to do the activity without everyone's help!

Hidden Objects

NUMBER OF PLAYERS ②

TIME NEEDED

20–30 minutes

You'll Need
● **Pencil**
● **Paper**
● **Colorful items**
(such as beads
or Easter eggs)

ACTIVITY OVERVIEW

Breaking a project into smaller steps is good. If different people can complete the smaller steps at the same time, that is even better. Completing smaller tasks together to finish one big task is called parallelism. Computer programmers use parallelism to make their code faster and easier to run. Computational thinkers use it to accomplish their work more efficiently. In this activity, you and a friend will use parallelism to find hidden objects.

INSTRUCTIONS

To start, hide small, colorful objects around your house. Ideas are Easter eggs, toys, or small colorful beads. Then, tell a friend that there are a number of objects that they should find. Have them look for the objects. As they find each hidden object, they should put a tally mark on a sheet of paper. Have them do this for every object until they find the last one. Once they're done, have your friend hide the objects so you can find them. After you've found all of the objects, think about what the task would have been like if you and another friend could work together to find the objects. Would it have been easier or harder? Taken shorter or longer? How would you have divided the work between the two of you? Write that plan on a sheet of paper. To build on this activity, you can get a few more friends together and make teams. Each team has to find the objects the other team hides.

Peek and Copy

NUMBER OF PLAYERS [2 OR MORE]

TIME NEEDED

20–30 minutes

ACTIVITY OVERVIEW

Computational thinkers often have to think through and repeat processes in order to finish tasks correctly. In this activity, you and some friends will try to copy a drawing.

You'll Need
- Pencil
- Drawing supplies
- Paper
- Stopwatch

INSTRUCTIONS

In this activity, ask some friends to help you! Each of you will get a piece of paper. One person will be the judge for the game. Before you begin, the judge draws a picture on their sheet of paper. They should hide the drawing by flipping the paper over. Everyone else should have drawing supplies and their own sheet of paper. The goal of this game is for someone to re-create the judge's drawing first. One at a time, all artists should look at the

judge's drawing for ten seconds. They have that much time to try to remember what they saw. After the ten seconds are up, each artist should use their memory to try to copy the drawing. The judge can show their drawing to each player more than one time. Each time, though, the artist can see the drawing for only ten seconds. You should repeat this with everyone individually until someone says they are done drawing. The judge then decides if the first finisher was close enough to their drawing to win. Once a player has won, the judge should show their drawing to everyone and ask the winner to explain how they were able to finish their copy first.

Conditional Diet

NUMBER OF PLAYERS **1**

TIME NEEDED

15–20 minutes

ACTIVITY OVERVIEW

A computer can only understand things as they are. This is called thinking literally. As humans, our words don't always express what we mean. Sometimes we exaggerate what we say. This is called figurative language. If/then statements, taken literally, can be a fun way of looking at the world! In this activity, you will imagine a common phrase literally.

INSTRUCTIONS

You might have heard the popular English phrase "You are what you eat." Now, think about your favorite food. After you have your favorite food in mind, draw a picture showing what you would look like if a computer read this and it thought you literally were what you ate. What would you look like as a slice of pizza? As a soft drink? As a cookie? To finish, underneath your drawing, complete the sentence: "IF I eat _____, THEN _____."

THINK ABOUT IT!

Computer programmers like to say that computers do exactly what you tell them to do. What they mean is that computers take things literally. Programmers have to be careful when they write code. They need to use the code to tell the computer everything it needs to know. The computer won't figure something out on its own. If something goes wrong with a computer program, it's probably because the coder forgot to tell the computer something, or the coder told the computer to do the wrong thing.

Color Change

NUMBER OF PLAYERS

TIME NEEDED

15–20 minutes

ACTIVITY OVERVIEW

If/then statements are good to know and understand. They happen in many parts of life. For example, IF it is cold outside, THEN you must wear a warm jacket. These statements are also called conditional statements, or conditionals. Computer programs have many conditionals in them. Thinking in conditionals lets a programmer create complex code that also runs smoothly. In this activity, you will learn about conditional changes in color.

INSTRUCTIONS

First, draw a pair of plain white shoes on a sheet of paper. Then, draw the shoes again—but this time, imagine what they would look like if the person wearing them had stepped in a big puddle of mud. Draw them with that in mind. After finishing this picture, write an if/then statement next to it. An example is, "IF someone steps in mud, THEN their shoes turn brown."

Repeat this exercise for all the colors in the rainbow. After each drawing, write a new if/then statement that explains why you're using a different color for each new picture.

Simon Conditionally Says

NUMBER OF PLAYERS **3 OR MORE**

TIME NEEDED

15–20 minutes

ACTIVITY OVERVIEW

There are many examples of if/then statements happening in both real life and programming. The most common examples are in games. Each rule of a game can be given as a simple if/then statement that defines how the game is supposed to work. In this activity, you and some partners will work together to change a classic game.

INSTRUCTIONS

For this activity, ask some friends for their help! Once at least three players are together, you will play the game of Simon Says. One person is Simon. Simon calls out instructions to the other players. Players only do what Simon tells them IF Simon says,

"Simon says," before the instruction. For example, IF Simon says, "Simon says scratch your head," THEN the players scratch their heads. IF Simon only says, "Scratch your head," THEN players who scratch their head are out.

Play a round of Simon Says. Then, work together to come up with your own version of the game! Using if/then statements, you and your friends should explore a new way of playing the game. For example, "IF a statement doesn't begin with 'Simon says,' THEN each player should do the opposite of the instructions." Then, play a round with your new rule!

IF I Write a Story

NUMBER OF PLAYERS

TIME NEEDED

20–30 minutes

ACTIVITY OVERVIEW

Many computer programs are made of if/then statements. If/then statements aren't just in computer programs, though. They are in real life too. Sometimes, if/then statements can tell a story. In this activity, you will write your own story with if/then statements.

INSTRUCTIONS

Have you ever read the book *If You Give a Mouse a Cookie*? If you have a copy or can get one, look at the words of the story. Do you notice a pattern? Every page has an if/then statement on it. In this activity, you will write your own story. The story should read like *If You Give a Mouse a Cookie,* but it should be about your life. Use as many if/then statements to tell the story as you can. To get started, you can use a statement such as: "IF I eat a whole pizza, THEN I will feel sick" or "IF we go to Florida for our family vacation, THEN we will all get a tan." By the end of the story, there should be at least ten if/then statements. When you're finished, read the story to someone out loud. You could even draw pictures for your book!

Rolling Conditionals

NUMBER OF PLAYERS **2**

TIME NEEDED

20–30 minutes

You'll Need
- Pencil
- Paper
- Pair of six-sided dice

ACTIVITY OVERVIEW

Computer programmers know if/then statements help programs work. They give the programs instructions to follow. They also help the program act a certain way. If/then statements can be used in other parts of life too. For example, in this activity, you will follow if/then statements to play a game.

INSTRUCTIONS

To start, get a pair of six-sided dice. Have a family member or friend play this game with you. The rules are: You roll the dice. IF you roll the same number on both dice (called **doubles**), THEN your family member or friend gets some kind of reward. Ideas for rewards are a piece of candy or extra time watching TV. Roll the dice a few times and reward your teammate if doubles come up. Remember, whether you roll doubles or not, certain things had to happen for the if/then statement to occur.

After playing this game for a few minutes, come up with a new game. Use if/then statements for the rules. For example, IF you roll certain numbers, certain combinations of numbers, or a certain total, THEN you will earn a certain number of points. Invent the game's rules and write them down. As you work, remember, your rules should always be written as if/then statements!

Character If/Then

TIME NEEDED

15–20 minutes

You'll Need
- Pencil
- Drawing supplies
- Paper

ACTIVITY OVERVIEW

All computational thinkers know how important if/then statements are to computer programs. If/then statements can help other parts of life too. For example, they can help describe characters. In this activity, you will use if/then statements to talk about a character you imagine.

INSTRUCTIONS

First, invent a **fictional** character. Then, draw a picture of your character and imagine what type of character they will be. Underneath your drawing, write out a set of if/then statements that describe your character. Statements could include:

IF _____ is hungry, THEN _____.

IF _____ goes to the park, THEN _____.

IF _____ doesn't go to bed on time, THEN _____.

Glossary

CODE Instructions that a computer follows to work.

COMPUTATIONAL THINKING A way of thinking where you break a big task into smaller tasks.

CONDITIONALS If/then statements.

DOUBLES Having the same number show up on two dice at the same time.

EFFICIENT Something that is easily or more simply done.

FICTIONAL Made-up; imaginary.

IF/THEN STATEMENTS Instructions that say if X happens, then Y happens as a result.

MELODY The main part of a piece of music that people sing.

PARALLEL COMPUTING A system of coding where multiple parts perform activities at the same time. Also called parallelism.

Find Out More

BOOKS

Loya, Allyssa. *Conditionals with Incredibles 2*. Disney Coding Adventures. Minneapolis, MN: Lerner Publishing, 2018.

Lyons, Heather. *Coding in the Real World*. Kids Get Coding. Minneapolis, MN: Lerner Classroom, 2017.

WEBSITE

Girls Who Code

https://girlswhocode.com

This website helps girls who are interested in coding get involved.

VIDEO

Hour of Code: Bill Gates Explains If/Then Statements

https://www.youtube.com/watch?v=m2Ux2PnJe6E

Computer businessman Bill Gates explains if/then statements.

Index

Entries in **boldface** are glossary terms.

code, 8, 12, 14, 19, 20

computational thinking, 5, 6, 12, 14, 16, 28

conditionals, 4–5, 18–19, 20–21, 22–23, 24–25, 26–27, 28–29

doubles, 26–27

efficient, 7, 8–9, 12, 14

fictional, 28

figurative language, 18–19

group activities, 6–7, 10–11, 14–15, 16–17, 22–23, 26–27

if/then statements, 4–5, 18–19, 20–21, 22–23, 24–25, 26–27, 28–29

If You Give a Mouse of Cookie, 24–25

individual activities, 8–9, 12–13, 18–19, 20–21, 24–25, 28–29

instructions, 4, 19, 26

literal thinking, 18–19

melody, 11

parallel computing, 5, 6–7, 8–9, 10–11, 12–13, 14–15

pattern, 11, 24

planning, 6–7, 8–9, 11, 15, 16

problem-solving, 5, 6, 10, 16–17

rules, 22–23, 26–27

teamwork, 5, 6–7, 8–9, 10–11, 12–13, 14–15

testing, 4, 7, 9, 13, 15